Wise Men Talking Series

LAO ZI Says

老子说

蔡希勤 编注

□责任编辑 **韩晖**

□翻译 **王琴 姜防震**

□绘图 **李士伋**

老人家说
系列丛书

华语教学出版社
SINOLINGUA

First Edition 2006
Second Printing 2007
Third Printing 2009

ISBN 978-7-80200-215-9

Published by Sinolingua
24 Baiwanzhuang Road, Beijing 100037, China
Tel: (86) 10-68320585
Fax: (86) 10-68326333
http://www.sinolingua.com.cn
E-mail: hyjx@sinolingua.com.cn
Printed by Beijing Foreign Languages Printing House
Distributed by China International Book Trading Corporation
35 Chegongzhuang Xilu, P. O. Box 399
Beijing 100044, China

Printed in the People's Republic of China

老人家说
Wise Men Talking

俗曰:“不听老人言,吃亏在眼前。”

老人家走的路多,吃的饭多,看的书多,经的事多,享的福多,受的罪多,可谓见多识广,有丰富的生活经验,老人家说的话多是经验之谈,后生小子不可不听也。

在中国历史上,春秋战国时期是中国古代思想高度发展的时期,那个时候诸子并起,百家争鸣,出现了很多“子”字辈的老人家,他们有道家、儒家、墨家、名家、法家、兵家、阴阳家,多不胜数,车载斗量,一时星河灿烂。

后来各家各派的代表曾先后聚集于齐国稷下学宫,齐宣王是个开明的诸侯王,因纳无盐丑女钟离春为后而名声大噪,对各国来讲学的专家学者不问来路一律管吃管住,享受政府津贴,对愿留下来做官的,授之以客卿,造巨室,付万钟。对不愿做官的,也给予“不治事而议论”之特殊待遇。果然这些人各为其主,各为其派,百家争鸣,百花齐放,设坛辩论,著书立说:有的说仁,有的说义,有的说无为,有的说逍遥,有的说非攻，有的说谋攻，有的说性善，有的说性恶，有的说亲非亲，有的说马非马，知彼知己，仁者无敌……留下了很多光辉灿烂的学术经典。

可惜好景不长，秦始皇时丞相李斯递话说“焚书坑儒”，结果除秦记、医药、卜筮、种树书外，民间所藏诗、书及百家典籍一把火烧个精光。到西汉武帝时，董仲舒又上了个折子，提出“罢黜百家，独尊儒术”，从此，儒学成了正统，“黄老、刑名百家之言”成为邪说。

“有德者必有言”，儒学以外的各家各派虽屡被扫荡，却不断变幻着生存方式以求不灭，并为我们保存下了十分丰富的经典著作。在这些经典里，先哲们留下了很多充满智慧和哲理的、至今仍然熠熠发光的至理名言，我们将这些各家各派的老人家的“金玉良言”编辑成这套《老人家说》丛书，加以注释并译成英文，采取汉英对照出版，以飨海内外有心有意于中国传统文化的广大读者。

As the saying goes, “If an old dog barks, he gives counsel.”

Old men, who walk more roads, eat more rice, read more books, have more experiences, enjoy more happiness, and endure more sufferings, are experienced and knowledgeable, with rich life experience. Thus, what they say is mostly wise counsel, and young people should listen to them.

The Spring and Autumn (722 – 481 BC) and Warring States (475 – 221 BC) periods of Chinese history were a golden age for ancient Chinese thought. In those periods, various schools of thought, together with many sages whose names bore the honorific suffix "Zi", emerged and contended, including the Taoist school, Confucian school, Mohist school, school of Logicians, Legalist school, Military school and Yin-Yang school. Numerous and well known, these schools of thought were as brilliant as the Milky Way.

Later representatives of these schools of thought flocked to the Jixia Academy of the State of Qi. Duke Xuan of Qi was an enlightened ruler, famous for making an ugly but brilliant woman his empress. The duke provided board and lodging, as well as government subsidies for experts and scholars coming to give lectures, and never inquired about their backgrounds. For those willing to hold official positions, the duke appointed them guest officials, built mansions for them and paid them high salaries. Those unwilling to take up official posts were kept on as advisors. This was an era when "one hundred schools of thought contended and a hundred flowers blossomed." The scholars debated in forums, and wrote books to expound their doctrines: Some preached benevolence; some, righteousness; some, inaction; some, absolute freedom; some, aversion to offensive war; some, attack by stratagem; some, the goodness of man's nature; some, the evil nature of man. Some said that relatives were not relatives; some said that horses were not horses; some urged the importance of knowing oneself and one's enemy; some said that benevolence knew no enemy... And they left behind many splendid classic works of scholarship.

Unfortunately, this situation did not last long. When Qin Shihuang (reigned 221 - 206 BC) united all the states of China, and ruled as the First Emperor, his prime minister, Li Si, ordered that all books except those on medicine, fortune telling and tree planting be burned. So, all poetry collections and the classics of the various schools of thought were destroyed. Emperor Wu (reigned 140 - 88 BC) of the Western Han Dynasty made Confucianism the orthodox doctrine of the state, while other schools of thought, including the Taoist and Legalist schools, were deemed heretical.

These other schools, however, managed to survive, and an abundance of their classical works have been handed down to us. These classical works contain many wise sayings and profound insights into philosophical theory which are still worthy of study today. We have compiled these nuggets of wisdom uttered by old men of the various ancient schools of thought into this series Wise Men Talking, and added explanatory notes and English translation for the benefit of both Chinese and overseas readers fond of traditional Chinese culture.

目录

CONTENTS

A

B

Refrain from exalting capable men, so that the people shall not compete.

不自见，故明〔10〕

He does not merely rely on his own eyes, therefore he is wise and penetrating.

C

持而盈之，不如其已〔12〕

To hold and fill is not as good as to give up.

宠辱若惊〔14〕

People love vanity so much as to be easily alarmed.

D

大道废，有仁义〔16〕

It is when the Great Way is abandoned that the doctrine of benevolence and righteousness arises.

大道甚夷，而民好径〔18〕

The highway is very even, but men are fond of the short cut.

大方无隅，大器晚成〔20〕

The greatest square has no corners; the greatest vessel takes the longest to finish...

大巧若拙，大辩若讷〔22〕

The greatest skill seems to be clumsy. The greatest eloquence seems to stammer.

道常无为而无不为〔24〕

The Tao invariably does nothing, and yet there is nothing left undone.

道可道，非常道〔26〕

The Tao that can be spoken of is not the eternal Tao.

道生一，一生二，二生三，三生万物〔28〕

The Tao gives birth to the unified thing (One), the One splits itself into two opposite aspects (Two), the Two gives birth to another (Three), the newborn Three produces the myriad things.

道生之，德畜之〔30〕

The Tao begets all beings, and De fosters them.

道者，万物之奥〔32〕

The Tao governs all things.

F

反者道之动〔34〕

Constant reversal is the movement of the Tao...

夫轻诺必寡信〔36〕

Light promising makes one lose one's credibility.

G

甘其食，美其服〔38〕

Let the people be contented with their food, pleased with their clothing...

谷神不死，是谓玄牝〔40〕

The Valley Spirit never dies. It is named the Mysterious Female.

故常无欲，以观其妙〔42〕

Therefore, he who rids himself forever of desire can see the subtleties of the Tao.

贵以身为天下，若可寄天下〔44〕

Only those who value themselves for the world can undertake its important tasks.

H

合抱之木，生于毫末〔46〕

A huge tree which fills one's arms grows from a small heap of earth.

惚兮恍兮，其中有象〔48〕

So vague and elusive is it, yet in it the form exists.

祸莫大于不知足〔50〕

There is no calamity greater than discontentment.

祸莫大于轻敌〔52〕

There is no disaster greater than underestimating the enemy.

祸兮，福之所倚〔54〕

It is upon bad fortune that good fortune leans.

J

见素抱朴，少私寡欲〔56〕

Manifest plainness，embrace simplicity，reduce selfishness and harbor few desires.

江海所以能为百谷王者〔58〕

The rivers and seas can become the leaders of many streams precisely because they stay in the lower valleys.

将欲歙之，必固张之〔60〕

What is in the end to be contracted，must first be expanded.

金玉满堂，莫之能守〔62〕

If your hall is filled with gold and jade，whoever could keep them safe?

居善地，心善渊〔64〕

He is at ease with lowness in his dwelling.

绝圣弃智，民利百倍〔66〕

Banish wisdom and discard knowledge, and the people will benefit a hundredfold.

K

抗兵相加，哀者胜矣〔68〕

If the forces of two sides are in balance,the side in grief will win.

孔德之容，惟道是从〔70〕

The content of great De is in conformity with the Tao.

M

民不畏死，奈何以死惧之〔72〕

Since the people do not fear death, what is the point of trying to frighten them with death.

民之从事，常于几成而败之〔74〕

People often fail when they are about to succeed in their work.

民之难治，以其上之有为〔76〕

The people are difficult to rule because the rulers are fond of taking action.

民之饥，以其上食税之多〔78〕

The people suffer from famine because the rulers gobble up too much tax-grain.

Q

曲则全，枉则直〔80〕

To yield is yet to be preserved wholly；to be bent is yet to become straight.

取天下常以无事〔82〕

To govern all under Heaven one usually should not take any arbitrary action.

R

人法地，地法天〔84〕

Man follows the way of Earth，Earth follows the way of Heaven. . .

弱之胜强，柔之胜刚〔86〕

The reason why the weak can overcome the strong and the soft can overcome the hard is known to all the people under Heaven.

S

善人者不善人之师〔88〕

The good man is the teacher of the bad，and the bad man is the material from which the good man learns.

善为士者不武〔90〕

He who is good at being an officer does not boast of his martial prowess.

善行，无辙迹〔92〕

One who is skilled at traveling leaves no trace of his wheels or footsteps.

善有果而已，不敢以取强〔94〕

Content yourself with your success, and stop; do not seek to dominate all under Heaven by force.

善者不辩，辩者不善〔96〕

A good man does not prove things by argument; he who proves things by argument is not good.

上善若水〔98〕

The highest good is like water.

上士闻道，勤而行之〔100〕

When the man of highest competency hears of the Tao, he diligently practices it.

生而不有，为而不恃〔102〕

To give birth to all things but not to take possession of them...

圣人处无为之事，行不言之教〔104〕

The sage manages affairs by "non-action," and teaches by "saying nothing".

圣人无常心，以百姓心为心〔106〕

The sage has no fixed personal will; he regards the people's will as his own.

圣人自知不自见〔108〕

The sage knows himself, but does not show himself.

师之所处，荆棘生焉〔110〕

Wherever armies are stationed, briers and thorns grow wild.

受国之垢，是谓社稷主〔112〕

He who bears the humiliation of the whole state can be the lord of the country.

T

太上，不知有之〔114〕

The best rulers are those about whom the people know nothing but their existence.

天长地久〔116〕

Heaven is eternal and Earth everlasting.

天得一以清，地得一以宁〔118〕

Heaven attained the Tao, and became clear. Earth attained the Tao, and became tranquil.

天地不仁，以万物为刍狗〔120〕

Heaven and Earth are ruthless, letting all things emerge or

perish of themselves.

天地相合，以降甘露〔122〕

Yin and Yang between Heaven and Earth unite to drip sweet dew.

天网恢恢，疏而不失〔124〕

The net of Heaven is vast. It has large meshes, but it lets nothing escape.

天下难事必作于易〔126〕

Everything difficult under Heaven must be dealt with while it is still easy.

天下莫柔弱于水，而攻坚强者莫之能胜〔128〕

Nothing under Heaven is softer and weaker than water, but in attacking the hard and strong, no force can compare with it. . .

天下皆知美之为美〔130〕

When all people under Heaven acknowledge the beautiful as beauty. . .

天下之至柔〔132〕

The softest thing under Heaven is able to run in and out of the hardest.

天之道，利而不害〔134〕

The Way of Heaven is beneficial to all things, and not harmful.

为学日益，为道日损〔136〕

The pursuit of learning may lead to the increase of desires day after day. The pursuit of the Tao is aimed at decreasing desires day after day.

为之于未有，治之于未乱〔138〕

Deal with things before they happen，and get things in order before the onset of their disorder.

我无为而民自化〔140〕

The sage said：“I do nothing，and the people of themselves submit. . . ”

无名，天地之始〔142〕

The nameless is the origin of Heaven and Earth.

物壮则老，是谓不道〔144〕

Things must grow old after reaching their prime，which is contrary to the Tao.

X

希言自然〔146〕

Saying few words fits in with Nature.

小国寡民〔148〕

Given a small country with few inhabitants.

信言不美，美言不信〔150〕

Sincere words are not fine, and fine words are not sincere.

Y

以道佐人主者，不以兵强于天下〔152〕

He who assists the ruler with the Tao does not dominate all under Heaven by force.

以身观身，以家观家〔154〕

Know a person in the perspective of a person, know a family in the perspective of a family.

以正治国，以奇用兵〔156〕

A state should be governed in a normal way, a war should be prosecuted in an unusual way.

用兵有言：吾不敢为主而为客〔158〕

A master of the art of war says, "I dare not take the offensive, but prefer to take the defensive..."

有国之母，可以长久〔160〕

Having the foundation of government, one can maintain sovereignty for a very long time.

有物混成，先天地生〔162〕

There was something formless yet complete that existed before Heaven and Earth.

有无相生，难易相成〔164〕

By opposing each other，existence and nonexistence come into being.

鱼不可脱于渊〔166〕

Fish cannot be taken away from deep water.

Z

躁胜寒，静胜热〔168〕

Rapid walking overcomes cold，and staying quiet overcomes heat.

执大象，天下往〔170〕

Whoever holds fast to the great image will become that one to whom all people under Heaven will come.

知常容，容乃公〔172〕

Only by knowing the eternal can one embrace all；only by embracing all can one be impartial；being impartial. . .

知其白，守其黑〔174〕

He who knows the white but keeps to the black is ready to be the model of all under Heaven.

知其荣，守其辱〔176〕

He who knows glory but keeps to disgrace. . .

知其雄，守其雌〔178〕

He who knows the masculine but keeps to the feminine. . .

知人者智，自知者明〔180〕

He who knows others is wise；he who knows himself is enlightened.

知我者希，则我者贵〔182〕

Those who are able to understand me are very few，and those who are able to follow me are very hard to meet.

知者不博，博者不知〔184〕

He who knows does not show off his learning，and he who shows off his learning does not know.

知者不言，言者不知〔186〕

He who knows does not speak，and he who speaks does not know.

知足不辱，知止不殆〔188〕

Whoever is contented will meet no disgrace，and whoever knows when and where to stop will meet no danger.

知足者富，强行者有志〔190〕

He who is content is rich；he who acts with persistence has will. . .

治大国若烹小鲜〔192〕

Governing a great state is like frying small fish (so frequent disturbance should be avoided).

治人事天莫如啬〔194〕

For the rule of the people and the service of Heaven, there is nothing better than the principle of inaction.

致虚极，守静笃〔196〕

Try to the utmost to make the heart vacant, and be sure to hold fast to quietude.

重为轻根，静为躁君〔198〕

The heavy is the root of the light, and the tranquil is the master of the active.

自见者不明，自是者不彰〔200〕

He who only relies on his own eyes cannot see clearly; he who considers himself always in the right cannot tell right from wrong.

老子说

LAO ZI SAYS

老子，姓李名耳，字聃，一说字伯阳。春秋末楚国人。古时有老氏而无李氏，故李耳即老耳。老子出世充满传奇色彩，不可详考。

老子初为周守藏室之史时，也曾“著书言治乱之事，以干世主”，史载孔子曾适周，问礼于他，孔子称他是“乘风云而上天的龙”。后见周室衰微，辞官西去。“至关，关令尹喜曰：‘子将隐矣，强为我著书。’于是老子乃修书上下篇，言道德之意五千余言而去，莫知其所终。”

老子主张“无为”，名言曰：“我无为而民自化，我好静而民自正，我无事而民自富，我无欲而民自朴。”“是以圣人处无为之事，行不言之教。”“治大国若烹小鲜。”“以正治国，以奇用兵，以无事取天下。”

Lao Zi's name was Li Er, with the courtesy name Dan (some say Boyang). He was a native of the State of Chu in the later years of Spring and Autumn Period. In ancient times, there was the surname Lao while no

Li, and thereby Li Er was Lao Er. The birth of Li Er was legendary and textual details could not be found.

When Lao Zi worked as an archivist in the Imperial Library of the Zhou Dynasty court, he "wrote books on how to deal with state disorder, so as to serve the ruler." Historical documents record that Confucius once went to the State of Zhou and discussed ritual and propriety with Lao Zi. Confucius called him "a dragon roaring to the heaven by wind and cloud." Later as the authority of Zhou's court was diminishing, Lao Zi resigned from his post and went westward. "When he reached a pass, the director said with joy, 'Since you are going to live in seclusion, would you write a book for me?' And then Lao Zi compiled a book of two volumes with more than 5,000 Chinese words expounding on Tao, and left with nobody knowing his whereabouts."

Lao Zi favored "non-action" and that "Non-action, and yet there is nothing that is not done by it." His famous sentences include: "I do nothing, and the people of themselves submit. I am fond of keeping still, and the people of themselves act righteously. I take no trouble, and the people enrich themselves. I have no desires, and the people naturally remain in primitive simplicity." "The sage manages affairs by non-action, and teaches by saying nothing." "Governing a great state is like frying small fish (so frequent disturbance should be avoided)." "A state should be governed in a normal way, a war should be prosecuted in an unusual way, and a kingdom should be controlled by doing nothing."

爱民治国，能无知乎？

Can you love the people and govern the state without personal knowledge?

爱民治国，能无知乎？

《老子》第10章

Can you love the people and govern the state without personal knowledge?

【注释】

无知：知，通“智”，智慧的意思，老子主张“无为”，所以他以“无以为”和“有以为”来分别上德和下德。在三十八章中说：“上德不德，是以有德；下德不失德，是以无德。上德无为而无以为；下德为之而有以为。”无为则无以为，有为则有以为。无以为则顺其自然，而德全，表虽不德，实则全德，故谓有德。有以为则显其所长，难免一偏，表虽不失德，实则其德不全，故谓无德。

【译文】

爱民治理国家，能够不用智慧吗？

兵强则灭，木强则折

An army will be shattered when it becomes strong; trees will snap when they grow strong.

兵强则灭，木强则折。强大处下，柔弱处上。

《老子》第76章

An army will be shattered when it becomes strong; trees will snap when they grow strong. The hard and strong are cast down; the soft and weak are set on high.

【注释】

兵强则灭，木强则折：奚侗《老子集解》曰："兵强则以杀伐为事，终致灭亡。各本多作'兵强则不胜'，非是。木强则失柔韧之性，易致断折。"

老子主张守柔处弱，不贵坚强。

【译文】

兵力强大反而会灭亡，树木高大就会折断。坚强开始向柔弱转化，故处于下降状态；柔弱开始向坚强转化，故处于上升状态。

不出户，知天下

Without going out of the door, one can know all things under Heaven.

不出户，知天下；不窥牖，知天道。

《老子》第47章

Without going out of the door, one can know all things under Heaven. Without looking out of the window, one can see the Way of Heaven.

【注释】

户：门。**窥**（kuī）：从里向外看。**牖**（yǒu）：窗。老子认为感性经验是靠不住的。在认识论上，他夸大了理性认识的作用。苏子由在《道德真经注》中说："天下之大，世俗之见有所眩而不知也；夫唯圣人出于万物之表，而揽其终始，得其大全。若夫世人不知道之全体，以耳目之所知为至，区区以察为明，至于察甚伤物，而不悟其非，可不哀哉？知小察之察不能尽物，而不用其能，恐其陷于一偏，而不及反也。"其实，老子这种夸大理性认识作用的方法，也同样是要"陷于一偏"的。

【译文】

足不出户，便知道天下大事；不向窗外看，就知道天的运行规律。

不尚贤，使民不争

Refrain from exalting capable men, so that the people shall not compete.

不尚贤，使民不争。不贵难得之货，使民不为盗。不见可欲，使民心不乱。

《老子》第3章

Refrain from exalting capable men, so that the people shall not compete. Refrain from valuing rare goods, so that the people shall not steal. Refrain from displaying anything arousing desire, so that the people's hearts will not be disturbed.

【注释】

不尚贤：尚，崇尚。尚贤，尊崇贤人。老子生活在春秋末期，天下大乱，诸侯国之间相互征伐，大国为兼并小国称霸诸侯，小国为应对大国而寻求自立。为此各诸侯国的统治者纷纷招揽贤才，作为安邦强国之计。当时的社会刮起一阵“尚贤”之风，然而“尚贤”的结果却给民间带来了莫大的灾难。针对当时社会上的“尚贤”主流，老子提出“不尚贤”的主张。《庄子·天地》：“至德之世，不尚贤，不使能。”但也有人认为“贤，多财也。”不尚贤，犹不尚多财，**难得之货：**金玉宝货。**为盗：**当盗贼。**不见可欲：**见，通“现”，显露。可欲，即多欲也。

【译文】

不尊崇贤才，使百姓之间就不会为功名利禄而引起争端。不以金玉财宝为贵，百姓就不会做盗贼。不显露那些能引起人们欲望的东西，可以使百姓心安不作乱。

不自见，故明

He does not merely rely on his own eyes, therefore he is wise and penetrating.

不自见，故明；不自是，故彰；不自伐，故有功；不自矜，故长。夫唯不争，故天下莫能与之争。

《老子》第22章

He does not merely rely on his own eyes, therefore he is wise and penetrating. He does not consider himself always in the right, therefore he is able to tell right from wrong. He does not boast about himself, therefore he is given credit. He does not think himself superior, therefore he is qualified for leadership. It is precisely because he does not compete that nobody under Heaven can compete with him.

【注释】

自伐，自矜：均为自夸，自我炫耀的意思。见《老子》第24章："自伐者无功，自矜者不长"。**夫唯不争**：河上公注曰："此言天下贤与不肖，无能与不争者也。""不争"是老子的处世哲学，和"无为"的主张一样。

【译文】

不自我表现，所以能名扬天下；不自以为是，所以才名声彰显；不居功自夸，所以功不可没；不自高自大，所以才能处人之上。正因为不与人争，因此谁也不能与他相争。

持而盈之，不如其已

To hold and fill is not as good as to give up.

持而盈之，不如其已；揣而锐之，不可常保。

《老子》第9章

To hold and fill is not as good as to give up. If a sword edge is sharpened to its sharpest extent, it will be hard for it to last long.

【注释】

持而盈之：做事要求圆满。持，握持，引申为做事。盈，满，有过度的意思，自满自骄都是“盈”的表现。凡事要求圆满，就免不了会有倾覆的祸患。所以老子告诫人们不可盈。**已：**停止。**揣（zhuī）而锐之：**捶锻而使之锐利，揣，捶击锻磨。锐，用作动词，使之锐。老子认为，不论做什么事都不可过度，而应该适可而止。锋芒毕露，而会招致灾祸。他希望人们把握好度，适可而止。

【译文】

办事要求过分圆满完美，不如停止不干；刀刃捶锻得太锋利，锋刃不能保持长久。

宠辱若惊

People love vanity so much as to be easily alarmed.

宠辱若惊，贵大患若身。

《老子》第 13 章

People love vanity so much as to be easily alarmed. And they consider great trouble as precious as their lives.

【注释】

宠辱若惊：受宠惊喜，受辱惊恐，受宠、受辱都心神不安。把失宠、受辱看作大患，像失掉自身（生命）一样。形容患得患失，与此相对成语是“宠辱不惊”。意谓对得宠或受辱都不动心，把得失置之度外。什么叫宠辱若惊呢？老子认为本来下贱的人得到宠爱会惊喜，失去宠爱会惊恐，受辱受宠都会心神不定，这就叫宠辱若惊。

【译文】

受宠、受辱都会惊慌失措，这是把祸患看得像生命一样重要。

大道废，有仁义

It is when the Great Way is abandoned that the doctrine of benevolence and righteousness arises.

大道废，有仁义。智慧出，有大伪。六亲不和，有孝慈。国家昏乱，有忠臣。

《老子》第18章

It is when the Great Way is abandoned that the doctrine of benevolence and righteousness arises. It is when knowledge and wisdom appear that the Great Hypocrisy emerges. It is when a family is out of harmony that filial piety and parental affection to children are advocated. It is when a country falls into disorder that loyal ministers appear.

【注释】

本章所谓仁义、大伪、孝慈、忠臣，都是由于君上失德而致。君上不失德，至德之世，人皆仁义，故仁义不见；及大道（正道）废弃，乃倡仁义之名以挽颓风。**六亲**：中国历史上对六亲说法不一。**昏乱**：君主昏暗，政治混乱。**忠臣**：忠贞之臣。

【译文】

大道废弃，才有所谓仁义。智慧出现，才有所谓诈伪。家庭不和睦，才有所谓孝慈。国家政治混乱，才有所谓忠臣出现。

大道甚夷，而民好径

The highway is very even, but men are fond of the short cut.

大道甚夷，而民好径。

《老子》第53章

The highway is very even, but men are fond of the short cut.

【注释】

夷：平也。**径**：山谷之间的崎岖小路，斜路。“而民好径”之民字，有的版本作“人”字。奚侗曰：“‘人’指人主言，各本皆误作‘民’，与下文谊不相属。盖古籍往往‘人’‘民’互用，以其谊可两通。此‘人’字属君言，自不能借‘民’为之，兹改正。‘径’，邪道也。”

【译文】

大路是平坦的，可是有人却偏喜欢走小（斜）路。

大方无隅，大器晚成

The greatest square has no corners; the greatest vessel takes the longest to finish...

大方无隅，大器晚成，大音希声，大象无形。道隐无名，夫唯道，善贷且成。

《老子》第41章

The greatest square has no corners; the greatest vessel takes the longest to finish; the greatest sound is faint; the greatest form looks formless. The Tao is hidden and nameless, yet it is only the Tao that supports all beings and brings them to fulfillment.

【注释】

隅（yú）：角。**大器晚成**：大器物总是最后完成。成语“大器晚成”出于此。器，指才干。成，成就。指能担当大事的人要经过长期的锻炼，所以成就较晚。**希**：无声。《老子》第14章：“听之不闻曰希。”**大象**：王弼注曰：“大象，天象之母也。”本指世间一切事物的本原。后也借指封建帝王的一统天下。**道隐无名**：道，无形无声。隐，无形，看不见。无名，不可名状。**贷**：施予，帮助。

【译文】

最大的方形没有角，最大的器物总是最后完成，最大的声音听来好像无声，最大的形象反而无形象。道虽然无形无声，不可名状，然而它却善于帮助万物并成就万物。

大巧若拙，大辩若讷。

The greatest skill seems to be clumsy. The greatest eloquence seems to stammer.

大巧若拙，大辩若讷。

《老子》第45章

The greatest skill seems to be clumsy. The greatest eloquence seems to stammer.

【注释】

巧：灵巧。**拙**：笨拙。《庄子·胠箧》："毁绝钩绳而弃规矩，擺工倕之指，而天下始人有其巧矣，故曰大巧若拙。"**大辩**：善于辩论。**讷**（nè）：语言迟钝，不善于讲话。

老子认为一个完美的人格，不在外形上表露，而为内在生命的含藏内收。

【译文】

真正灵巧的人表面上倒像很笨拙的样子，有口才善于辩论的人表面上好像语言迟钝，不善于讲话的样子。

道常无为而无不为

The Tao invariably does nothing, and yet there is nothing left undone.

道常无为而无不为。侯王若能守之，万物将自化。

《老子》第37章

The Tao invariably does nothing, and yet there is nothing left undone. If dukes and kings can preserve it, all things will submit to them spontaneously.

【注释】

道常无为：蒋锡昌曰："道常者，道之真，一章所谓'常道'也。'无为'者，言其体；'无不为'者，言其用。"**自化**：自我化育发展。老子认为，从道分出万物，并不是由于"道"的有目的、有意识的作为，"道"是无目的、无意识的。就其无目的、无意识来说，"道"是"无为"的；就其生长万物说，"道"是"无不为"的。这就是所谓"道常无为而无不为"。

【译文】

道永远是无为的，然而却又成就了天下所有的事物。诸侯君主若能遵循这个原则，天下万物将自我化育发展。

道可道，非常道

The Tao that can be spoken of is not the eternal Tao.

道可道，非常道；名可名，非常名。

《老子》第1章

The Tao that can be spoken of is not the eternal Tao; the name that can be named is not the eternal name.

【注释】

道：《老子》书中的道，一般指支配物质世界或现实事物运动变化的普遍规律，有时也专指物质世界的实体，亦即宇宙本体。“道”字本来是指人走的道路，有四通八达的意思。这一意义引申为“方法”、“途径”，已初步地具有规律性、普通性的意思。**可道：**可，可以。道，说。**常道：**即永恒不变的规律。常，永恒。原作“恒”，为避汉孝文帝刘恒讳，改“恒”为“常”。**名：**与“道”对称。即永恒不变的名。**可名：**可以叫得出的名字，也就是具体事物的名字。

【译文】

可以说得出具体形态的道，就不是永恒不变的道了；可以叫得出具体特性的名，就不是永恒不变的名了。

道生一，一生二，二生三，三生万物

The Tao gives birth to the unified thing (One), the One splits itself into two opposite aspects (Two), the Two gives birth to another (Three), the newborn Three produces the myriad things.

道生一，一生二，二生三，三生万物。万物负阴而抱阳，冲气以为和。

《老子》第42章

The Tao gives birth to the unified thing (One), the One splits itself into two opposite aspects (Two), the Two gives birth to another (Three), the newborn Three produces the myriad things. The myriad things have Yin and Yang within themselves as opposing forces. Yin and Yang interact and are unified into harmony in Qi (vital energy).

【注释】

一：某一种事物。《老子》本章中的“一”、“二”、“三”历来解释分歧很大。一，指道；二，指阴阳二气；三，指阴阳二气互相作用而成的和气。《易·系辞》则称一为“太极”，二为“两仪”（天地）“天地合而生和，二生三也。和气合而生物，三生万物也。”**负阴而抱阳：**包含着阴和阳两个对立面。“负”和“抱”都是包含的意思。**冲气：**阴阳二气相互激荡。

【译文】

“道”产生一，一产生二，二产生三，三产生万物。万物皆包含着阴阳两个相反的方面，阴阳二气互相激荡得到统一。

道生之，德畜之

The Tao begets all beings, and De fosters them.

道生之，德畜之，物形之，势成之。是以万物莫不尊道而贵德。

《老子》第51章

The Tao begets all beings, and De fosters them. The Tao and De give them form, and the environment makes them accomplished. Therefore, all beings without exception venerate the Tao and value De.

【注释】

之：代指万物。**德**：在老子哲学中的“道”和“德”和儒家学说中的“道”和“德”属于不同的范畴。老子认为“道”的属性表现为“德”，“德”是“道”在人世间的体现，“道”是客观规律，而“德”是指人类认识并按客观规律办事。**畜**（xù）：养。**形之**：使万物成形。形，使动用法。**势**：环境。

【译文】

道产生万物，德养育万物并使万物成形，环境使万物完成。因此天下万物没有不尊崇道而重视德的。

道者，万物之奥

The Tao governs all things.

道者，万物之奥，善人之宝，不善人之所保。美言可以市尊，美行可以加人。

《老子》第62章

The Tao governs all things. It is treasured by good men, and is also preserved by bad men. Eloquent words can purchase honor from others, and admirable deeds can put one above others.

【注释】

奥：主。《礼记·礼运》："人情以为田，故人以为奥也。"注："奥犹主也，田无主则荒。"**所保**：所以安身的东西。保，保护，引申为安。**市**：买卖，此处指买，获取，得到。**加人**：居于人上。

【译文】

道是天下万物的主宰者，是善人的法宝，也是不善人借以安身的东西。美好的言词可以获取别人的尊敬，漂亮的行为可以出人头地。

反者道之动

Constant reversal is the movement of the Tao. . .

反者道之动。弱者道之用。天下万物生于有，有生于无。

《老子》第40章

Constant reversal is the movement of the Tao, and being weak is the function of the Tao. All things under Heaven come into being from visible concrete beings, and all beings come into being from the invisible Tao.

【注释】

反：复也。王弼说："复者，反本之谓也。"**天下万物生于有，有生于无**：有，存在的物质。无，虚无的空间，即"道"。

【译文】

向着相反的方向变化，是"道"的运行规律。保持着柔弱的状态，是"道"的作用。天下万物生于可见的具体事物，可见的具体事物都是从看不见的"道"中产生。

夫轻诺必寡信

Light promising makes one lose one's credibility.

夫轻诺必寡信，多易必多难。

《老子》第63章

Light promising makes one lose one's credibility, and thinking things easy leads to difficulty.

【注释】

诺（nuò）：答应、许诺。**寡信**：缺少信用。后成语“轻诺寡信”出于此。意谓轻易许诺，不守信约。**易**：用作动词，把事情看得容易。

老子认为，做任何事情都是从小到大，由少到多，由易到难的。

【译文】

轻率许诺必缺少信用，把事情看得太容易，必会遇到许多的困难。

甘其食，美其服

Let the people be contented with their food, pleased with their clothing...

甘其食，美其服，安其居，乐其俗。邻国相望，鸡犬之声相闻，民至老死不相往来。

《老子》第 80 章

Let the people be contented with their food, pleased with their clothing, satisfied with their homes, and delight in their plain customs. The neighboring states are within sight of each other, and the crowing of cocks and barking of dogs can be heard by one another. But the people do not have any contact with each other throughout their long lives.

【注释】

甘：用如使动词。“甘其食”即“使其食甘。”使他们吃好。下面“美”、“安”、“乐”的用法相同。

【译文】

使老百姓以粗茶淡饭为香甜，以粗布衣服为华美，以简居陋俗为安乐。相邻的国家离得很近，相互望得见，连鸡鸣犬吠也听得到，但老百姓却直到老死彼此不相往来。

谷神不死，是谓玄牝

The Valley Spirit never dies. It is named the Mysterious Female.

谷神不死，是谓玄牝。玄牝之门，是谓天地之根。

《老子》第6章

The Valley Spirit never dies. It is named the Mysterious Female. And the Doorway of the Mysterious Female is the base from which Heaven and Earth sprang.

【注释】

谷神：道的神奇作用。河上公本注："谷，养也。"**玄牝**（pìn）：道家指衍生万物的本源。蒋锡昌曰："玄者，幽远微妙之意。'牝'，母也，为生物之本。'玄牝'者，即微妙之生长，以谷神生之而不见其所以生也。"

【译文】

道的神妙作用永不会消失，它好像一个玄妙的母体。玄妙母性之门，是产生天地万物的根源。

故常无欲，以观其妙

Therefore, he who rids himself forever of desire can see the subtleties of the Tao.

故常无欲，以观其妙；常有欲，以观其徼。

《老子》第1章

Therefore, he who rids himself forever of desire can see the subtleties of the Tao; he who has never rid himself of desire can see only the superficiality of the Tao.

【注释】

常无欲：常。原作“恒”，盖为避汉孝文帝刘恒讳。**欲**：志欲、情欲，包括善恶、爱憎、喜怒，所谓七情六欲皆是也。**妙**：指天地万物的微妙之处。**徼**（jiào）：边界，引申为表面。

【译文】

所以如果能保持清静无欲，就可以观察天地万物的微妙之处；如果贪欲太多，就只可以看到天地万物的表面现象。

贵以身为天下，若可寄天下

Only those who value themselves for the world can undertake its important tasks.

贵以身为天下，若可寄天下；爱以身为天下，若可托天下。

《老子》第13章

Only those who value themselves for the world can undertake its important tasks. Only those who love the world above themselves can be entrusted with the rule of it.

【注释】

贵以身为天下：情愿把自己的全部身心投入到治理天下工作中去的人。贵，看重，引伸为愿意。以，用。为，治理。**若可：**才可。若，乃，才。**寄：**委托。《论语·泰伯》："可以托六尺之孤，可以寄百里之命。"

【译文】

只有那些情愿把自己全部身心投入到治理天下工作中去的人，才可以把天下交给他；只有那些爱天下胜过爱自身的人，才可以把天下托付给他。

合抱之木，生于毫末

A huge tree which fills one's arms grows from a small heap of earth.

合抱之木，生于毫末；九层之台，起于累土；千里之行，始于足下。

《老子》第64章

A huge tree which fills one's arms grows from a small heap of earth; a high terrace which has nine storeys rises from a small heap of earth; a journey of a thousand li begins with the first step.

【注释】

毫末：毛的尖端，比喻细小。毫，长而尖锐的毛。**累**：同“蔂”，装土的筐子。高亨《老子正诂》：“起于累土，犹言起于蒉土也。”**千里之行**：有本作“千仞之高”。意为“登上千仞高山，必从脚下第一步开始”，亦可通。

【译文】

合抱的大树，是由细小的萌芽长成的；九层高台，是从第一筐土筑起来的；千里长行，是从第一步开始的。

惚兮恍兮，其中有象

So vague and elusive is it, yet in it the form exists.

惚兮恍兮，其中有象。恍兮惚兮，其中有物。

《老子》第21章

So vague and elusive is it, yet in it the form exists. So profound and obscure is it, yet within it are entities.

【注释】

恍惚（huǎnghū）：老子在无与有之间，用恍惚来表示道体，使道成为恍惚抽象、虚无缥缈不可言状的存在，往往使人产生无中生有的错觉。但这个道是有内容的，所以老子讲“惚兮恍兮，其中有象。恍兮惚兮，其中有物。”这句话是说道之为物，是恍惚的，但恍惚之中，却有象、有物。

【译文】

在恍惚迷离之中，却有形象。在迷离恍惚之中，却有实体。

祸莫大于不知足

There is no calamity greater than discontentment.

祸莫大于不知足，咎莫大于欲得。故知足之足，常足矣。

《老子》第46章

There is no calamity greater than discontentment. There is no guilt greater than covetousness. Therefore the contentment with knowing contentment is always contented.

【注释】

咎（jiù）：灾难。**常足**：人没有过多的贪求就能时常觉得满足。成语“知足常乐”出于此，常与“能忍自安”连用。

老子认为引起战争的主要原因是执政者贪欲太多，解决问题的办法是使执政者知足常乐。

【译文】

最大的灾祸是不知道满足，最大的危险是贪得无厌。所以知道满足的这种满足，才能永远感到满足。

祸莫大于轻敌

There is no disaster greater than underestimating the enemy.

祸莫大于轻敌，轻敌几丧吾宝。

《老子》第69章

There is no disaster greater than underestimating the enemy, and underestimating the enemy nearly makes me lose my "three precious things."

【注释】

轻敌几丧吾宝：苏辙曰："圣人以慈为宝，轻敌则轻战；轻战则轻杀人，丧其所以为慈矣。"丧，丧失，引申为违背。吾宝，这里指三宝（一慈，二俭，三不敢为天下先）实际指道。"几丧吾宝"意思是如果轻易与人为敌，这基本上是违背了道的原则。

【译文】

灾祸莫大于轻易树敌，轻易树敌就违背了道的原则。

祸兮，福之所倚

It is upon bad fortune that good fortune leans.

祸兮，福之所倚；福兮，祸之所伏。

《老子》第58章

It is upon bad fortune that good fortune leans, and upon good fortune that bad fortune rests.

【注释】

祸兮，福之所倚：倚（yǐ），靠。老子的本意是说“祸福相生”。祸与福相互依存，可以相互转化。汉·贾谊《鹏鸟赋》：“祸兮福所倚，福兮祸所伏，忧喜聚门兮，吉凶同域。”亦作“祸福相倚”。有成语叫“福为祸始”，也叫“祸为福先”。意为享福太甚常隐伏祸机，受尽灾祸之后可能好运会降临。由此形成的成语还有“祸与福邻”“祸中有福”、“祸作福阶”、“祸福相倚”、“祸绝福连”、“福过灾生”等。

【译文】

灾祸里隐藏着幸福；幸福里隐伏着灾祸。

见素抱朴，少私寡欲

Manifest plainness, embrace simplicity, reduce selfishness and harbor few desires.

见素抱朴，少私寡欲。

《老子》第19章

Manifest plainness, embrace simplicity, reduce selfishness and harbor few desires.

【注释】

见素抱朴：焦竑《老子翼》引吕吉甫注："见素抱朴，少私寡欲，乃其所属也。见素，则知其无所与杂而非文；抱朴，则知其不散而非不足。素而不杂，朴而不散，则复乎性，而外物不能惑，而少私寡欲矣。少私寡欲，而后可以语绝学之至道也。"老子要求统治者修养到无为、无事、无欲和好静的境界，不务虚华之事，不逐身外之利。《颜氏家训·勉学》："古人之贵义轻财，少私寡欲，忌盈恶满，赒穷恤匮。"

【译文】

行为单纯，内心淳朴；减少私心，降低欲望。

江海所以能为百谷王者

The rivers and seas can become the leaders of many streams precisely because they stay in the lower valleys.

江海所以能为百谷王者，以其善下之，故能为百谷王。

《老子》第66章

The rivers and seas can become the leaders of many streams precisely because they stay in the lower valleys. So they can be the leaders of many streams.

【注释】

百谷王：谷，小河流。蒋锡昌曰："《说文》：'泉出通川为谷'，是'百谷'犹百川也。《说文》：'王，天下所归往也'，是'王'即归往之义。此言江海所以能为百川归往者，以其善居卑下之地，故能为百川归往也。61章王注：'江海居大而处下，则百川流之'，即据此文而言。"**下之**：居于河流之下。之，代指"百谷"。

【译文】

江海所以能成为百川汇聚处，是由于它处于百川的下游，所以能成为百川汇聚处。

将欲歙之，必固张之

What is in the end to be contracted, must first be expanded.

将欲歙之，必固张之；将欲弱之，必固强之；将欲废之，必固兴之；将欲夺之，必固与之。

《老子》第36章

What is in the end to be contracted, must first be expanded. Whatever is to be weakened, must begin by being strengthened. What is to be destroyed, must first be promoted. He who would be a taker, must begin as a giver.

【注释】

歙（xī）：一本作翕，古通用字。《说文》："歙，缩鼻也。"有收缩义，与"张"相对。**固**：一本作姑，马叙伦曰："固，读为姑且之姑。"

【译文】

要想使其收缩，必先使之扩张；要想削弱它，必先加强它；要相废除它，必先振兴它；要想夺取它，必先给予它。

金玉满堂，莫之能守。

If your hall is filled with gold and jade, whoever could keep them safe?

金玉满堂，莫之能守。富贵而骄，自遗其咎。功成身退，天之道。

《老子》第9章

If your hall is filled with gold and jade, whoever could keep them safe? Wealth and position breed insolence, that brings ruin in turn. To withdraw as soon as the work is done, that is the Way of Heaven.

【注释】

金玉满堂：也作金玉盈堂、金玉满室。谓财富极多，后亦用以称人富有才学。**富贵而骄**：富贵而骄傲。**功成**：成功。**天道**：自然规律。《荀子·天论》："天有常道矣，地有常数矣。"古人认为天道是支配人类命运的天神意志。

【译文】

黄金美玉堆满屋宇，没有人能守得住传给子孙后代。富贵而傲慢，是自取灾祸。事业成就后引身告退这是合乎天道的。

居善地，心善渊

He is at ease with lowness in his dwelling.

居善地，心善渊，与善仁，言善信，正善治，事善能，动善时。

《老子》第8章

He is at ease with lowness in his dwelling. He is profound in his heart. He is sincere in his dealings with others. He is faithful in speech. He is orderly in government. He is competent in deeds. He is timely in action.

【注释】

居善地：意即在位，如水之好趋下让人。**心善渊**：渊，深也。意谓心好深藏如渊。**与善仁**：乐于助人，像水一样令人可亲。**言善信**：信守诺言，像水那样真诚。**正善治**：为政精简像水一样清静。**事善能**：办事圆通，像水一样顺遂。**动善时**：行动善于随时变化，像水一样一往无前。

【译文】

安居于卑下之地，思想虚静深沉，交往仁慈友爱，讲话诚信无欺，为政清静安定，做事无所不能，行为择时而动。

绝圣弃智，民利百倍。

Banish wisdom and discard knowledge, and the people will benefit a hundredfold.

绝圣弃智，民利百倍。绝仁弃义，民复孝慈。绝巧弃利，盗贼无有。

《老子》第19章

Banish wisdom and discard knowledge, and the people will benefit a hundredfold. Banish benevolence and discard morality, and the people will return to filial piety and parental affection. Banish skill and discard profit, and thieves and robbers will disappear.

【注释】

绝圣弃知：这体现了老子的“无为而治”的思想，要求圣人（执政者）返到“恒无欲”的境界，天下自然就太平了。

智慧是人们的向往与追求，但老子则认为知慧是人们痛苦的源泉。老子的主张无疑带有愚民倾向，但它的主观愿望是为了保持人民头脑单纯，心灵朴实，即保持人民完整的自然境界。

【译文】

抛弃聪明才智，百姓可以获利百倍。抛弃仁义，百姓就能回复孝慈的美德。抛弃技巧和私利，盗贼就不会产生。

抗兵相加，哀者胜矣。

If the forces of two sides are in balance, the side in grief will win.

抗兵相加，哀者胜矣。

《老子》第69章

If the forces of two sides are in balance, the side in grief will win.

抗兵相加：抗兵，举兵。抗，举。王弼注："抗，举也。"加，施加，这里指把兵力施加于敌方，也即攻敌。《孙子·九地》："威加于敌，故其城可拔。"**哀者**：王弼注："哀者必相惜，而不趣利避害，故必胜。"哀兵，受压而悲愤的军队。意思是反对战争，又受到攻击，不得已而进行自卫反击，自然是带着悲哀心情的，这样军队能够取胜。成语"哀兵必胜"出于此，后多指被压迫而从事正义战争的一方，一定会胜利。苏辙曰："两敌相加，而吾出于不得已，则有哀心。哀心见而天人助之，虽欲不胜，不可得也。"

【译文】

两军对阵兵力相当，受压抑而奋起反抗的一方必定胜利。

孔德之容，惟道是从。

The content of great De is in conformity with the Tao.

孔德之容，惟道是从。道之为物，惟恍惟惚。

《老子》第21章

The content of great De is in conformity with the Tao. The thing that is called the Tao has no definite form.

【注释】

孔德：大德。孔，大。德，品质。**容：**动容，容止。也有解为内容，含义。也通。**惟道是从：**即“惟从道”的意思。惟，同唯，仅仅。从，遵循。**惟恍惟惚：**恍惚的意思。隐约不清，难以捉摸的样子。

【译文】

大德之人的一举一动，都是和道保持一致。道这个东西，是看不见，摸不着的。

民不畏死，奈何以死惧之？

Since the people do not fear death, what is the point of trying to frighten them with death.

民不畏死，奈何以死惧之？

《老子》第74章

Since the people do not fear death, what is the point of trying to frighten them with death?

【注释】

宋·张耒《老子议》：“故曰‘民不畏死，奈何以死惧之’，苟为畏死耶！”常用以表示不怕死之气概。苏辙曰：“政烦刑重，民无所措手足，则常不畏死。虽以死惧之，无益也。”

老子认为，执政者所施行的苛政和酷刑，滥杀百姓，人民并不能被压服。

【译文】

老百姓不怕死，怎么能用死来威胁他们呢？

民之从事，常于几成而败之

People often fail when they are about to succeed in their work.

民之从事，常于几成而败之。慎终如始，则无败事。

《老子》第64章

People often fail when they are about to succeed in their work. If they are as careful in the end as at the beginning, they will not ruin their work.

【注释】

几：将要。贾谊《论积贮疏》："汉之为汉，几四十年矣。"**慎终**：谨慎小心，始终如一。**败事**：把事情办坏。

老子认为，无论做什么事情，不仅要有坚强的毅力，从小处做起，而且还必须谨慎小心，始终如一，才能成就大事业。

【译文】

人们做事，常常在快要成功的时候失败了。如果谨慎小心，始终如一，就不会把事情办坏。

民之难治，以其上之有为

The people are difficult to rule because the rulers are fond of taking action.

民之难治，以其上之有为，是以难治。

《老子》第75章

The people are difficult to rule because the rulers are fond of taking action. Thus they are difficult to rule.

【注释】

有为：有所作为。老子主张“无为而治”，所以反对执政者的“有为”，他认为统治者好大喜功，大搞土木建筑、侵伐征战等多所作为是难以治理好老百姓的。

【译文】

老百姓所以难以治理，是因为统治者太好有所作为了，所以老百姓才难以治理。

民之饥，以其上食税之多

The people suffer from famine because the rulers gobble up too much tax-grain.

民之饥，以其上食税之多，是以饥。

《老子》老 75 章

The people suffer from famine because the rulers gobble up too much tax-grain. Thus they suffer from famine.

【注释】

上：指统治者。此句下为："民之难治，以其上之有为，是以难治。民之轻死，以其上求生之厚，是以轻死。"意谓反映了人民与统治者之间阶级矛盾的实质：人民的饥饿，是统治者沉重的租税造成的；人民的反抗，是统治者苛酷压迫造成的；人民的轻生，是统治者贪得无厌的聚敛造成的。

【译文】

老百姓之所以吃不饱，就是因为统治者收税太多了，所以才吃不饱。

曲则全，枉则直

To yield is yet to be preserved wholly；to be bent is yet to become straight.

曲则全，枉则直；洼则盈，敝则新。

《老子》第22章

To yield is yet to be preserved wholly; to be bent is yet to become straight. To be hollow is yet to be filled up; to be worn out is yet to be renewed.

【注释】

曲则全：在当时激烈的阶级斗争中，老子主张“辞让”、“退智”的态度，也就是“曲全”，实际还是“无为”。《庄子·天下》述老子之道说：“人皆求福，己独曲全。”成语“委曲求全”即从此衍化而来，也作“委曲成全”、“委曲周全”。**枉则直**：枉，弯曲。成语“矫枉过正”是说矫正弯曲的东西超过了限度。**洼**：低洼之处。**敝**：破，旧。**新**：更新。

【译文】

委曲可以保全，弯曲可以伸直；低洼之处可以盈满，破败陈旧可以更新。

取天下常以无事

To govern all under Heaven one usually should not take any arbitrary action.

取天下常以无事，及其有事，不足以取天下。

《老子》第48章

To govern all under Heaven one usually should not take any arbitrary action. If one tends to do anything arbitrary, one is not qualified to govern all under Heaven.

【注释】

取：治理。**无事**：清静无为。**及**：如果，同“若”。据王引之《经传释词》，古时“及”、“若”通用。**不足**：不能。

老子认为具有清静无为，没有私欲妄见的人才可以治理国家。

【译文】

治理天下要依靠清静无为，如果碌碌多为，就不能够治理好天下。

人法地，地法天

Man follows the way of Earth, Earth follows the way of Heaven...

人法地，地法天，天法道，道法自然。

《老子》第25章

Man follows the way of Earth, Earth follows the way of Heaven, Heaven follows the way of the Tao, and the Tao follows the way of itself.

【注释】

人：通行本作“王”。唐·李约《道德真经新注》对这段话有不同的断句和注释。李约曰：“王（一作人）者，法地法天法道之三自然妙理而理天下也，故曰‘王法地地，法天天，法道道，法自然。’言法上三大之自然妙理也。其义云‘法地地’，如地之无私载；‘法天天’，如天之无私覆；‘法道道’，如道之无私生而已矣，如君君、臣臣、父父、子子之例也。”**自然**：本身的样子。自，指道本身。

【译文】

人效法地，地效法天，天效法道，道效法自然。（地无私载，人应效法地的无私；天无私覆，地应效法天的无私；道生而不有，为而不恃，长而不宰，天应效法道的无私；道则效法自然的无为之理，所以人应效法自然的无为）。

弱之胜强，柔之胜刚

The reason why the weak can overcome the strong and the soft can overcome the hard is known to all the people under Heaven.

弱之胜强，柔之胜刚，天下莫不知，莫能行。

《老子》第78章

The reason why the weak can overcome the strong and the soft can overcome the hard is known to all the people under Heaven. But none follow and practice it.

【注释】

弱之胜强，柔之胜刚：老子以水为喻说明柔克刚、弱胜强的道理。蒋锡昌曰："此言水之道，柔弱可以胜刚强，天下莫不知，然竟莫能行也。七十章：'天下莫能知，莫能行'，则指圣人之道言，故文字与此稍异。盖圣人之道，知难行难；而水之道，知易行难也。"

【译文】

弱胜强，柔克刚，天下没有人不知道这个道理，但就是没有人实行它。

善人者不善人之师

The good man is the teacher of the bad, and the bad man is the material from which the good man learns.

善人者不善人之师，不善人者善人之资。不贵其师，不爱其资，虽智大迷。是谓要妙。

《老子》第27章

The good man is the teacher of the bad, and the bad man is the material from which the good man learns. He who does not honor his teacher and who does greatly care for the material is greatly confused though he thinks himself wise. Such is the subtle essence.

【注释】

资：资助、凭藉的意思。孔子说："三人行，必有我师焉。择其善者而从之，其不善者而改之。"（《论语·述而》）也是这个意思。**贵师、爱资**：善者为师，恶者为资，这是事物所包涵的对立的两个方面。**要妙**：即微妙要道。"这里指善人为不善人之师，不善人为善人之资，善与不善互为转化，这就叫做微妙的要道。

【译文】

善人是不善人的老师，不善人是善人的鉴戒。如果不尊重老师，不爱惜鉴戒，即使是智慧者也会大迷不悟。这就是为人处事微妙的要道。

善为士者不武

He who is good at being an officer does not boast of his martial prowess.

善为士者不武，善战者不怒，善胜敌者不与，善用人者为之下。

《老子》第68章

He who is good at being an officer does not boast of his martial prowess; he who is good at fighting does not resort to rage; he who is skilful at defeating enemies does not wrestle with them; and he who is skilful at managing his men has a modest attitude toward them.

【注释】

士：古代文人、武人皆称“士”，这里指武士，一说指将官。王弼注：“士，卒之帅也。”**不武**：不表现勇武。武，勇猛，勇敢。《诗经·郑风·羔裘》：“孔武有力。”**不怒**：不会被激怒。**不与**：不争。与，对付。这里指与敌人作战。**为之下**：处人之下。为，处，居。之，代指所用的人。

【译文】

善于带兵的人不尚勇武，善于作战的人不容易被敌人激怒，善于致胜的人不会依靠攻伐，善于用人的人先对人表示谦下。

善行，无辙迹

One who is skilled at traveling leaves no trace of his wheels or footsteps.

善行，无辙迹；善言，无瑕谪。

《老子》第27章

One who is skilled at traveling leaves no trace of his wheels or footsteps; one who is skilled at speaking says nothing that can be found fault with.

【注释】

瑕谪：一本作“瑕适”。适、谪古通用。《管子·水地》：“夫玉瑕适皆见，精也。”尹注：“瑕适，玉疵也。”这是老子“无为而治”的权术。奚侗注曰：“仿佯尘垢之外，倏然而往，侗然而来，故无辙迹。”又说：“行不言之教，故无瑕谪。”老子本意是说治理天下要顺乎自然天性，使天下无为而治。

【译文】

善于行走，不会留下车迹；善于言谈者，不会留下破绽。

善有果而已，不敢以取强

Content yourself with your success, and stop; do not seek to dominate all under Heaven by force.

善有果而已，不敢以取强。果而勿矜，果而勿伐，果而勿骄，果而不得已，果而勿强。

《老子》第30章

Content yourself with your success, and stop; do not seek to dominate all under Heaven by force. Succeed but don't boast about it, succeed but don't brag about it, succeed but don't be arrogant, succeed and take it as you have to, succeed and don't attempt to dominate.

【注释】

果：胜利。《尔雅·释诂》："果，胜也。"**取强**：逞强。**矜**（jīn）：自大。**伐**：夸功。

【译文】

只要战胜敌人就罢手，不敢靠武力逞强。胜而不自大，胜而不居功自夸，胜而不骄傲，把胜利看作是不得已而为之，这就是取胜而不逞强的意思。

善者不辩，辩者不善

A good man does not prove things by argument; he who proves things by argument is not good.

善者不辩，辩者不善。

《老子》第81章

A good man does not prove things by argument; he who proves things by argument is not good.

【注释】

善者：善人，儒家指有道德的人。《论语·述而》："善人，吾不得而见之矣。"道家指善良之人，好人，得道之人。因善人止于真理，故不巧辩。**辩**：辩论，有口才。《孟子·滕文公下》："予岂好辩哉？予不得已也。"引申为巧言，诡辩。故老子说"辩者不善"。

老子这句话也有人解释为："善者不多言，多言者不善。"

【译文】

得道之人不巧辩，善于巧辩的人不是得道者。

上善若水

The highest good is like water.

上善若水。水善利万物而不争，处众人之所恶，故几于道。

《老子》第8章

The highest good is like water. Water is apt to benefit all things, and does not compete with them. It dwells in places people disdain. Thus it is closest to the Tao.

【注释】

上善若水：上善，最完美，至善。蒋锡昌《老子校诂》："上善，谓上善之人，即圣人也。"上善若水，即上善的人犹同水一样，而水德则近于道。王夫之说："五行之体，水为最微。善居道者，为其微，不为其著；处众之后，而常得众之先。"（《老子衍》）意思是常人之情，"人往高处走"正好与水性相反，此亦反证上善之人（圣人）若水也。

【译文】

道德高尚的人的言行就像水一样。水滋润万物而不与万物争利，它总是处在众人所厌恶的低洼之地，所以说它的行为基本上符合道的原则。

上士闻道，勤而行之

When the man of highest competency hears of the Tao, he diligently practices it.

上士闻道，勤而行之；中士闻道，若存若亡；下士闻道，大笑之，不笑，不足以为道。

《老子》第 41 章

When the man of highest competency hears of the Tao, he diligently practices it. When the man of average competency hears of the Tao, he half believes it. When the man of low competency hears of the Tao, he laughs loudly at it. If he didn't laugh, it would not qualify to be the Tao.

【注释】

上士：高明之士。**中士**：中等人。**下士**：最差一等的人。老子这里把士分为上、中、下三等，指其理解能力高下和各自“闻道”后的态度。**勤**：积极努力。**若存若亡（wú）**：若有若无。亡，同“无”。**大笑之**：大，用如意动词，认为“道”迂阔而不切合实际。笑，嘲笑。

【译文】

高明之士听说道，就努力去实行；普通人听说道，会将信将疑；粗俗之人听说道，会嘲笑它，如果道不被这种人嘲笑就不足以成其为道了。

生而不有，为而不恃

To give birth to all things but not to take possession of them...

生而不有，为而不恃，长而不宰，是谓玄德。

《老子》第51章

To give birth to all things but not to take possession of them, to raise them but not to vaunt this as its merit, and to be their sovereign but not to control them. These are called the profound De.

【注释】

生而不有：道生养万物而不将万物据为己有。**为而不恃**：帮助万物而不依赖它们。为，帮助。**长而不宰**：成就万物却不做它们的主宰。宰，主宰者。**玄德**：高尚的品德。玄，高深，高尚。《庄子·天地》："其合缗缗，若愚若昏，是谓玄德，同乎大顺。"

【译文】

道生养了万物却不将万物据为己有，抚育了万物却不居功恃能，成就了万物而不做它们的主宰，这才是最高尚的品德。

圣人处无为之事，行不言之教

The sage manages affairs by "non-action," and teaches by "saying nothing".

圣人处无为之事，行不言之教。

《老子》第2章

The sage manages affairs by "non-action," and teaches by "saying nothing".

【注释】

处无为之事：老子主张"无为而治"，他认为圣人处无为之事，并不是什么事都不做，而是要以无为的态度来处理世事，一任自然，就是要按照自然法则，让"万物作焉而不辞，生而不有，为而不恃，功成而弗居。"（《老子》第2章）**行不言之教**：无为而治，不用言辞教化，使民自化。《庄子·知北游》："夫知者不言，言者不知，故圣人行不言之教。"

【译文】

圣人所做的事就是顺应自然不提倡人为，不用空洞的言辞教化而使民自化。

圣人无常心，以百姓心为心

The sage has no fixed personal will; he regards the people's will as his own.

圣人无常心，以百姓心为心。

《老子》第49章

The sage has no fixed personal will; he regards the people's will as his own.

【注释】

无常心：没有永恒不变的思想。也可解为“没有私心”。苏辙曰：“虚空无形，因万物之形以为形，在方为方，在圆为圆，如始空自有形，则何以形万物哉？是以圣人无心，因百姓之心以为心。”

【译文】

执政者没有永恒不变的思想，而是以老百姓的思想作为自己的思想。

圣人自知不自见

The sage knows himself, but does not show himself.

圣人自知不自见，自爱不自贵。

《老子》第72章

The sage knows himself, but does not show himself. He knows his own value but does not put himself on high.

【注释】

见：同“现”，表现。蒋锡昌曰：“‘自知’与‘自爱’词异谊同，‘自见’与‘自贵’词异谊同。‘自爱’即清静寡欲；‘自贵’即有为多欲。此言圣人清静寡欲，不有为多欲，故去后者而取前者也。”

老子认为，理想的执政者应该不自居高贵，而要自知、自爱，抛弃自见和自贵。

【译文】

圣人有自知之明而不自我显示，有自爱之心而不自我抬高。

师之所处，荆棘生焉

Wherever armies are stationed, briers and thorns grow wild.

师之所处，荆棘生焉；大军之后，必有凶年。

《老子》第30章

Wherever armies are stationed, briers and thorns grow wild. Great wars are always followed by famines.

【注释】

所处：所驻扎过的地方。**大军**：这里指大战。**凶年**：灾荒年。

老子是反对战争的，他描绘的战乱图景是凄凉的，但他却并不像墨子那样疾呼“非攻”，也不像孟子那样诅咒：“善战者服上刑”，而只说“善战者果而已矣。”意谓“善于用兵的人能果敢决断就行了，不要以武力逞强。”

【译文】

军队驻扎过的地方，必然会土地荒芜，荆棘丛生；战争之后，必有灾荒之年。

受国之垢，是谓社稷主

He who bears the humiliation of the whole state can be the lord of the country.

受国之垢，是谓社稷主。受国不祥，是谓天下王。

《老子》第78章

He who bears the humiliation of the whole state can be the lord of the country. He who bears the disaster of the whole state can be the king of all under Heaven.

【注释】

垢（gòu）：屈辱。**社稷**（jì）：国家。社是土神，稷是谷神，由于历代王朝建立时都要立社稷而祭祀土地和五谷神灵，因此社稷也成了国家的代称。

【译文】

能够承担国家的屈辱，才算是天下的君主；能够承担国家的灾难，才算是天下的君王。

太上，不知有之

The best rulers are those about whom the people know nothing but their existence.

太上，不知有之；其次亲而誉之；其次，畏之；其次，侮之。

《老子》第17章

The best rulers are those about whom the people know nothing but their existence. The next best are those whom the people love and praise. The next best are those whom the people fear. The worst are those whom the people despise.

【注释】

太上：最上，指最好的统治者。**侮**：轻慢。

老子把统治者分为四种，他认为最理想的统治者是让人民不知道他的存在，最坏的统治者是被人民所轻侮，处在中间状态的两种统治者或是人民亲近并称赞他，或是害怕他。

【译文】

最好的人君，老百姓感觉不到他的存在；差一等的人君，老百姓亲近他、称赞他；再差一等的人君，老百姓害怕他；最次的人君，老百姓轻慢他。

天长地久

Heaven is eternal and Earth everlasting.

天长地久。天地所以能长且久者，以其不自生，故能长生。

《老子》第7章

Heaven is eternal and Earth everlasting. Heaven and Earth can be eternal and everlasting because they don't exist for themselves, and for this reason they obtain longevity.

【注释】

天长地久： 老子以天道推论人道，要人道效法天道。“天地”一词说明天道的关系。天地是指客观存在的大自然而言，自然界的一切事只须依照客观的发展规律运动生长好了，不再需要任何主宰者驾临其上来加以命令安排。（张松如《老子校读》）后只是把“天长地久”作为一个“长久”的时间概念来用。

【译文】

天长生，地久寿。天地之所以能够长生久寿，就在于它们不是为自己而存在，所以能够长生久寿。

天得一以清，地得一以宁

Heaven attained the Tao, and became clear. Earth attained the Tao, and became tranquil.

天得一以清，地得一以宁，神得一以灵，谷得一以盈，万物得一以生，侯王得一以为天下贞。

《老子》第39章

Heaven attained the Tao, and became clear. Earth attained the Tao, and became tranquil. Spirits attained the Tao, and became divine. Valleys attained the Tao, and became full. All things attained the Tao, and became luxuriant, and kings and princes attained the Tao and became the heads of all things under Heaven.

【注释】

得一：得道。《老子》中的"一"有三义：一指道；二指道所产生的最初的统一物。老子说："道生一，一生二，二生三，三生万物。"其"一"即此义；三指身。这里一指"道"，得一即得道。**贞**：同正，首领。

【译文】

天得道而清明，地得道而安宁，神得道而灵验，河谷得道而充盈，万物得道而能生养繁殖，诸侯君王得道而能治理天下。

天地不仁，以万物为刍狗

Heaven and Earth are ruthless, letting all things emerge or perish of themselves.

天地不仁，以万物为刍狗；圣人不仁，以百姓为刍狗。

《老子》第5章

Heaven and Earth are ruthless, letting all things emerge or perish of themselves. The sage too is ruthless, letting all people live or die by themselves.

【注释】

刍狗：河上公注曰："天地生万物，人为最贵，天地视之，如草刍狗畜；圣人视百姓，如草刍狗畜。"一说，古代祭祀所用茅草扎成的狗形，祭后则弃去。

【译文】

天地没有偏爱，任凭万物自然生长；理想的执政者没有偏爱，任凭百姓自作自息，繁衍生存。

天地相合，以降甘露

Yin and Yang between Heaven and Earth unite to drip sweet dew.

天地相合，以降甘露，民莫之令而自均。

《老子》第32章

Yin and Yang between Heaven and Earth unite to drip sweet dew. Without any command from the people, it drips evenly over all.

【注释】

天地相合，以降甘露：天之气和地之气相互交融而降下甘露。这属于“天人感应”思想。古人认为，社会政治清明，就会影响自然界。**民莫之令**：即“民莫令之”，没有人指使它。**自均**：自然均平。

【译文】

天地阴阳之气相交融而降下甘露，没有人指使它，而能自然均平。

天网恢恢，疏而不失。

The net of Heaven is vast. It has large meshes, but it lets nothing escape.

天网恢恢，疏而不失。

《老子》第73章

The net of Heaven is vast. It has large meshes, but it lets nothing escape.

【注释】

天网：天道。今多指法纪。**恢恢**：广大的样子。河上公本注："恢恢，甚大。"**疏**：稀。天道像个巨大的网，网孔看起来很稀疏，但决不会放过作恶的坏人。后用以形容作恶者逃脱不了国法惩处。后连用多作"天网恢恢，疏而不漏。"亦作"天道恢恢"。

【译文】

天网广大无边，网孔虽稀疏却不会有所漏失。

天下难事必作于易

Everything difficult under Heaven must be dealt with while it is still easy.

天下难事必作于易，天下大事必作于细。

《老子》第63章

Everything difficult under Heaven must be dealt with while it is still easy. Everything great under Heaven must be dealt with while it is still small.

【注释】

《韩非子·喻老》："有形之类，大必起于小；行久之物，族必起于少。故曰：'天下之难事必作于易，天下之大事必作于细'。是以欲制物者于其细也。故曰：'图难于其易也，为大于其细也'。"这是一种朴素辩证的方法论，隐含着事物由量变到质变的飞跃的法则。

【译文】

天下的难事必从容易事作起，天下的大事必从小事作起。

天下莫柔弱于水，而攻坚强者莫之能胜

Nothing under Heaven is softer and weaker than water, but in attacking the hard and strong, no force can compare with it...

天下莫柔弱于水，而攻坚强者莫之能胜，其无以易之。

《老子》第78章

Nothing under Heaven is softer and weaker than water, but in attacking the hard and strong, no force can compare with it, for nothing can take its place.

【注释】

莫之能胜：即“莫能胜之”。**无以易之**：没有什么可以代替它。无以，没有什么。易，代替。劳健《古本考》曰：“按此句诸本互异，‘易’之解亦各自为义。王弼注：‘无物可以易之’，谓更易也。玄宗注：‘万变而常一’，谓变易也。河上注：‘攻坚强者，无以易于水’，谓容易也。”

老子以水为喻，说明柔能胜刚、弱能胜强的道理。

【译文】

天下最柔弱的东西莫过于水，但攻破坚强的东西却没有能胜过水的，也没有一种东西可以替代它的。

天下皆知美之为美

When all people under Heaven acknowledge the beautiful as beauty. . .

天下皆知美之为美，斯恶已；皆知善之为善，斯不善已。

《老子》第2章

When all people under Heaven acknowledge the beautiful as beauty, there appears ugliness. When they acknowledge goodness as good, there appears evil.

【注释】

美之为美，斯恶已：恶者，丑也。老子认为一切事物都有自己的对立面，失去其中的一方，另一方也就不存在了。事物都是一分为二，二又共处于一之中，矛盾着的两个方面，互相依存，又互相转化。这就决定了既有“美”，就同时也就有了“丑”（恶）；既有“善”，就同时也就有了“不善”。“美”和“丑”（恶）是一对矛盾着的两个方面，当人们还不知道美的时候也就不知道什么是丑，当天下人都知道美之为美的时候，也同时知道了丑之为丑了。

【译文】

天下人都知道美的东西为美，就是已经有丑的东西了；天下都知道善之为善，就是已有不善存在了。

天下之至柔

The softest thing under Heaven is able to run in and out of the hardest.

天下之至柔，驰骋天下之至坚。

《老子》第43章

The softest thing under Heaven is able to run in and out of the hardest.

【注释】

驰骋：奔驰。**至坚**：最坚硬的东西。这是老子“柔之胜刚、弱之胜强”的思想。

【译文】

天下最柔弱的东西，能够穿行于最坚硬的东西里面。

天之道，利而不害

The Way of Heaven is beneficial to all things, and not harmful.

天之道，利而不害。圣人之道，为而不争。

《老子》第81章

The Way of Heaven is beneficial to all things, and not harmful. The Way of the sage is to compete against nobody in what he does.

【注释】

天之道：天道，天的运行规律。**利而不害**：施利于万物而不伤害万物。**圣人之道**：有的版本作“人之道”，和“天之道”相对应。

【译文】

天道是施利于万物而不伤害万物。圣人的处世原则是只帮助别人而不与人争利。

为学日益，为道日损

The pursuit of learning may lead to the increase of desires day after day. The pursuit of the Tao is aimed at decreasing desires day after day.

为学日益，为道日损，损之又损，以至于无为。无为而无不为。

《老子》第48章

The pursuit of learning may lead to the increase of desires day after day. The pursuit of the Tao is aimed at decreasing desires day after day. Decreasing and decreasing again, till one has reached non-action. Non-action, and yet there is nothing that is not done by it.

【注释】

为学：研究学问，指仁义礼智等学问。**益：**增加。**损：**减少。

老子认为外在的经验知识（仁义礼智等）积累愈多，私欲妄见也就层出不穷。只有“为道”，才能不断去除私欲妄见，使人日渐返朴归真，最终达到“无为”的境地。

【译文】

研究学问，情欲就会一天一天地增加；研究“道”，情欲就会一天一天地减少，减少再减少，最后达到清静无为地境界。清静无为反而能够成就一切事物。

为之于未有，治之于未乱

Deal with things before they happen, and get things in order before the onset of their disorder.

为之于未有，治之于未乱。

《老子》第64章

Deal with things before they happen, and get things in order before the onset of their disorder.

【注释】

为：动词，做准备。

老子认为，大的事物总是从小的事情上发展起来的，任何事物的出现，总有自身生成、变化和发展的过程，人们应该了解这个过程，防微杜渐，以防备事物朝大的祸患发展。

【译文】

在事情还没有发生的时候就做好准备，在国家还没有发生祸乱的时候就注意治理。

我无为而民自化

The sage said: "I do nothing, and the people of themselves submit..."

我无为而民自化，我好静而民自正，我无事而民自富，我无欲而民自朴。

《老子》第57章

The sage said: "I do nothing, and the people of themselves submit. I am fond of keeping still, and the people of themselves act righteously. I take no trouble, and the people enrich themselves. I have no desires, and the people naturally remain in primitive simplicity."

【注释】

老子提出"无为"、"好静"、"无事"、"无欲"的治国方案。老子把他的自然界的"无为"的发展法则运用到人类的社会上来，认为人类社会应同自然界一样，也须任之以"无为"，使其各遂其生，各顺其长，这就否定了人类社会的特殊性，否定了人类的社会实践对促进人类社会发展的重大意义，他的复古主义思想，正是从这里演绎出来的。(张松如《老子校读》)

【译文】

(圣人说)我无为老百姓自然归化，我清静老百姓自然端正，我无事老百姓自然能富足，我无欲老百姓自然淳朴。

无名，天地之始

The nameless is the origin of Heaven and Earth.

无名，天地之始；有名，万物之母。

《老子》第1章

The nameless is the origin of Heaven and Earth; the named is the foundation of all things.

【注释】

无名：道家指天地形成前的状名，指道。王弼注曰：“凡有皆始于无，故未形无名之时，则为万物之始。及其有形有名之时，则长之育之，亭之毒之，为其母也。”**始：**指开端。**有名：**这里亦指道而言。奚侗说：“无名有名皆谓道，天地之始，未立道名。”

【译文】

无名，是天地的开端；有名，是万物的本源。

物壮则老，是谓不道

Things must grow old after reaching their prime, which is contrary to the Tao.

物壮则老，是谓不道，不道早已。

《老子》第30章

Things must grow old after reaching their prime, which is contrary to the Tao. Whatever is contrary to the Tao will soon perish.

【注释】

物壮则老：物，存在于天地间的万物统称。壮，强壮。物壮则老，意同物极则反。谓事物发展到极度时，就会走向反面。**不道**：不遵循事物发展的规律。**早已**：快速灭亡。

【译文】

事物强盛到极点就会走向衰败，一味强行使事物强盛起来，这样不遵循“道”的原则，反而会使它过早地走向衰亡。

希言自然。

Saying few words fits in with Nature.

希言自然。故飘风不终朝，骤雨不终日。孰为此者？天地。天地尚不能久，而况于人乎。

《老子》第23章

Saying few words fits in with Nature. Therefore, a whirlwind does not last a whole morning, nor does a rainstorm last a whole day. What makes them like this? It is Heaven and Earth. Even Heaven and Earth cannot last long, how much less can man?

【注释】

希言自然:希言,字面意思是讲话很少,引申为清静无为。老子用自然界的狂风暴雨不能持久的事实作比喻,告诫当政者要实行"清静无为"的政治,而不要以强法严令横加干涉老百姓的生活,更不能施行暴政。**飘风:**旋风,狂风。**终朝:**整整一个早上。**为此:**产生狂风暴雨。为,产生。

【译文】

清静无为才合乎自然法则。所以说旋风不能刮一早上,暴雨不能下一整天。谁产生的狂风暴雨？是天地。天地尚且不能长时间维持狂风暴雨的状态,何况于人呢？

小国寡民

Given a small country with few inhabitants.

小国寡民，使有什佰之器而不用，使民重死而不远徙。

《老子》第 80 章

Given a small country with few inhabitants, though there are various kinds of instruments, let them not be used. Let the people not risk their lives, and not move to distant places.

【注释】

小国寡民：小、寡都用如动词，使国小、使民少。**什佰之器：**各种器具。什佰，即十百，泛指众多。**重死：**把死亡看得很重，重视生命。**徙**（xǐ）：搬迁。小国寡民是老子的理想社会，这个社会的特点是：国家小，人民少。

【译文】

国家小，百姓少，即使有许多器具也不使用，使老百姓看重生命而不轻易向远方迁移。

信言不美，美言不信。

Sincere words are not fine, and fine words are not sincere.

信言不美，美言不信。

《老子》第 81 章

Sincere words are not fine, and fine words are not sincere.

【注释】

信：诚实，不欺。《论语·学而》：“与朋友交而不信乎?”信实之言多尚朴直，故不美。**美言**：浮华之词。因多尚华饰，故不信。“美言不信”成语出于此。谓词藻华美的言辞、文章，内容往往不真实。

【译文】

真实的话不好听，好听的话不真实。

以道佐人主者，不以兵强于天下

He who assists the ruler with the Tao does not dominate all under Heaven by force.

以道佐人主者，不以兵强于天下。

《老子》第30章

He who assists the ruler with the Tao does not dominate all under Heaven by force.

【注释】

佐：帮助，辅佐。**以兵强天下：**靠武力逞强于天下。这一章是老子讲用兵之道的，“最下用兵以杀，其上用兵以生。”（王夫之语）有人认为《老子》八十一章，“未尝有一章不属意于兵也。”（唐·王真《道德真经论兵要义述》）近代章太炎认为《老子》一书概括了古代兵书的要旨。

【译文】

用道来辅佐君主的人，不以武力逞强于天下。

以身观身，以家观家

Know a person in the perspective of a person, know a family in the perspective of a family.

以身观身，以家观家，以乡观乡，以邦观邦，以天下观天下。

《老子》第54章

Know a person in the perspective of a person, know a family in the perspective of a family, know a neighborhood in the perspective of a neighbourhood, know a state in the perspective of a state, and know a kingdom in the perspective of a kingdom.

【注释】

以身观身：用修身的原则来观察个人。以，用。又蒋锡昌曰："'以身观身'，言以修道之身，观不修道之身，孰得孰失，孰存孰亡也。下四句文谊，依此类推。"

【译文】

用修身的原则来观察个人，用齐家的原则观察全家，用理乡的原则观察全乡，用治国的原则观察全国，用平天下的原则观察天下。

以正治国，以奇用兵

A state should be governed in a normal way, a war should be prosecuted in an unusual way.

以正治国，以奇用兵，以无事取天下。

《老子》第57章

A state should be governed in a normal way, a war should be prosecuted in an unusual way, and a kingdom should be controlled by doing nothing.

【注释】

正：正确的方法。老子的本意指“清静无为之道”。**奇**：邪。老子的本意指“权诈之术”。**无事**：老子本意指无为而治。**取**：治理。

【译文】

以正道治理国家，以奇术用兵作战，以清静无为的政策来治理天下。

用兵有言：吾不敢为主而为客

A master of the art of war says, "I dare not take the offensive, but prefer to take the defensive..."

用兵有言：吾不敢为主而为客，不敢进寸而退尺。

《老子》第69章

A master of the art of war says, "I dare not take the offensive, but prefer to take the defensive; I dare not advance an inch, but prefer to retreat a foot."

【注释】

主：主动进攻别人。**客**：被动地防守。苏辙曰："主，造事者也；客，应敌者也。进者，有意于争者也；退者，无意于争者也。"老子主张用兵之道，不取攻势而取守势；宁愿后退不肯冒进。这是以守为攻，以退为进的政治策略和用兵之道。表现了老子反对战争的思想，同时也表明老子处世哲学中的退守、居下原则。

【译文】

古时善于用兵的人说过：我不敢取攻势而宁愿取守势，不敢轻易冒进一寸却宁愿后退一尺。

有国之母，可以长久

Having the foundation of government, one can maintain sovereignty for a very long time.

有国之母，可以长久。是谓深根固柢，长生久视之道。

《老子》第59章

Having the foundation of government, one can maintain sovereignty for a very long time. This is called the Way in which one can plant the roots deep, make the stalks firm and maintain a long life.

【注释】

有国之母：有了治国的根本。母，根本，也即道。《韩非子·解老》："所谓有国之母，母者道也。"**深根固柢**（dǐ）：柢，树根。《说文》："柢，根也。"**久视**：与"长生"同义。

【译文】

掌握了治国的根本原则，就可以永远长存。这就是深根固柢，永世长存的道理。

有物混成，先天地生

There was something formless yet complete that existed before Heaven and Earth.

有物混成，先天地生。寂兮寥兮，独立不改，周行而不殆，可以为天地母。

《老子》第25章

There was something formless yet complete that existed before Heaven and Earth. Soundless and formless, it depends upon nothing external, and operates in a circular motion ceaselessly. It may be considered the root of all beings under Heaven.

【注释】

混成：混然而成。**寂兮寥兮**：寂，无声。寥，无形。**周行**：循环运动。**殆**：同怠，懈怠，引申为停止。**母**：根本，基本。

【译文】

有一物形成于混沌中，出现在天地形成之前。它无声无形，独立存在永不改变，循环运行永不停止，可以把它称为天地万物产生的基础。

有无相生，难易相成

By opposing each other, existence and nonexistence come into being.

有无相生，难易相成，长短相形，高下相倾，音声相和，前后相随。

《老子》第2章

By opposing each other, existence and nonexistence come into being, difficult and easy form themselves, long and short are distinct, high and low are contrasted, sound and voice harmonize, and front and back emerge.

【注释】

老子认为一切对立的事物，实际上是互相依存、联立并生的。对立事物的本身是互相含蕴的，即任何一方都含有对方的因素。**相生**：相互对立中产生。**相成**：相互形成。**相形**：相互比较。**相倾**：相互依赖。**相和**：相互区分。

【译文】

有和无在相互对立中得以发生，难和易在相互对应中得以形成，长和短在相互比较中得以显现，高和下在相互依赖中得以存在，音和声在相互应和中得以区分，前和后在相互对比中得以出现。

鱼不可脱于渊

Fish cannot be taken away from deep water.

鱼不可脱于渊，国之利器不可以示人。

《老子》第36章

Fish cannot be taken away from deep water, and effective weapons of state cannot be easily displayed to others.

【注释】

国之利器：一说指治国之权谋。河上公注："利器，权道也。"一说指人君赏罚之权，所以控制臣下者也。《韩非子·喻老》："故曰：'鱼不可脱于渊。'赏罚者，邦之利器也。在君则制臣，在臣则胜君。"鱼若脱于渊，则失去其生机；国之利器示于人，则丧其权势。

【译文】

鱼不能离开水，国家优良的武器不可以让别人知道。

躁胜寒，静胜热

Rapid walking overcomes cold, and staying quiet overcomes heat.

躁胜寒，静胜热，清静为天下正。

《老子》第45章

Rapid walking overcomes cold, and staying quiet overcomes heat. By remaining quiet and tranquil, one will be the chief of all under Heaven.

【注释】

躁（zào）：躁动，运动。**正**：长官，首领。奚侗转引徐大椿曰："凡事相反则能相制。如人躁甚则虽寒亦不觉，而足以胜寒；心静则虽热亦不觉，而足以胜热。由此推之，则天下纷纷纭纭，若我用智术以相逐，则愈乱而不可理矣；惟以清静处之，则无为而自化，亦如静之胜热矣。"

【译文】

运动可以战胜寒冷，安静可以克服炎热，清静无为的人可以统一天下。

执大象，天下往

Whoever holds fast to the great image will become that one to whom all people under Heaven will come.

执大象，天下往。往而不害，安平泰。

《老子》第35章

Whoever holds fast to the great image will become that one to whom all people under Heaven will come. Even if all people under Heaven come to him they will not hinder each other, and all will enjoy comfort, peace and health.

【注释】

象：道也。蒋锡昌《校诂》曰："'大象'即指大道而言。盖以道有法象，可为人君之法则，故谓大道为'大象'也。'执大象，天下往'，谓圣人守大道，则天下万民归往也。河上公注'执，守也。象，道也。圣人守大道，则天下万物移心归往之也。'" **往而不害**：是"万民不害圣人"还是"圣人不害万民"，有两种不同的说法。**安平泰**：三字同义，都是太平安乐的意思。

【译文】

执政者掌握了"道"，天下百姓就会归附于他，归附于他老百姓就不会受到伤害，就能过上太平安乐的生活。

知常容，容乃公

Only by knowing the eternal can one embrace all; only by embracing all can one be impartial...

知常容，容乃公，公乃王，王乃天，天乃道，道乃久，殁身不殆。

《老子》第16章

Only by knowing the eternal can one embrace all; only by embracing all can one be impartial; being impartial, you can be kingly; being kingly, you can be one with Nature; being one with Nature is in accord with the Tao; being in accord with the Tao is everlasting, and you can be free from danger throughout your life.

【注释】

容：包容。包容一切，包括生死、强弱、荣辱等。**公**：公正，正确。**王**（wàng）：称王，这里指治理国家的原则。**天**：指天道，自然规律。**殁**（mò）：死。**殆**（dài）：危险。

【译文】

懂得了这个永远不变的道理就能包容一切，能够包容一切就能够公正对待一切。能够公正对待一切就能懂得治国的原则，懂得了治国的原则，进而就能了解自然规律。了解了自然规律，进而就能掌握道。掌握了道，就能长久生存，终身不会遇到危险。

知其白，守其黑

He who knows the white but keeps to the black is ready to be the model of all under Heaven.

知其白，守其黑，为天下式。

《老子》第28章

He who knows the white but keeps to the black is ready to be the model of all under Heaven.

【注释】

知其白，守其黑： 河上公注曰："白以喻昭昭，黑以喻默默。人虽自知昭昭明达，当复守之以默默，如暗昧无所可。如是则可为天下法式，则其德常在。"意谓内心虽知是与非，但要安于沉默。这是古代道家主张无为的处世态度。这句话也有人释为：知道什么是显赫，却安于低下的地位。成语"知白守黑"出于此。

【译文】

心里非常明白，却安于暗昧状态，以做天下人的榜样。

知其荣，守其辱

He who knows glory but keeps to disgrace...

知其荣，守其辱，为天下谷。

《老子》第28章

He who knows glory but keeps to disgrace, is ready to be the valley under Heaven.

【注释】

荣：荣耀。**辱**：卑辱。**谷**：山谷，比喻低下的地位。《庄子·天下》篇引老聃曰："知其雄，守其雌，为天下溪。知其白，守其辱，为天下谷。"成玄英疏："是以去彼显白之荣华，取此韬光之屈辱，斯乃学道之机枢，故为宇内之豁谷也。"这是老子用柔弱、退守的原则来保身处世，并要求"圣人"也能如此治国安民。

【译文】

知道什么是荣耀，却安守卑辱的地位，其胸怀如同川谷一样博大。

知其雄，守其雌

He who knows the masculine but keeps to the feminine...

知其雄，守其雌，为天下溪。

《老子》第28章

He who knows the masculine but keeps to the feminine is ready to be the ravine under Heaven.

【注释】

知其雄，守其雌：雄，雄健，刚强。雌，雌柔，软弱。**溪：**河沟，比喻低下的地位。成语“知雄守雌”出于此。宋·范仲淹《老子犹龙赋》：“知雄守雌，宛讶存身之际；绝圣弃智，潜疑勿用之时。”

【译文】

知道什么是雄强，却安守雌柔的地位，其胸怀像沟溪一样宽广。

知人者智，自知者明。

He who knows others is wise; he who knows himself is enlightened.

知人者智，自知者明。胜人者有力，自胜者强。

《老子》第33章

He who knows others is wise; he who knows himself is enlightened. He who conquers others is physically strong; he who conquers himself is mighty.

【注释】

自知：自己了解自己。**明**：聪明；明察。成语："自知之明"出于此，指有正确认识自己的能力。

这是老子讲精神修养的话。老子认为，"知人""胜人"固然重要，而"自知""自胜"尤其重要。

【译文】

能了解别人的人是有智慧的人，能认识自己的人才是聪明的人。能战胜别人的人一定是有力量的人，能战胜自己的人才是坚强的人。

知我者希，则我者贵

Those who are able to understand me are very few, and those who are able to follow me are very hard to meet.

知我者希，则我者贵。是以圣人被褐怀玉。

《老子》第70章

Those who are able to understand me are very few, and those who are able to follow me are very hard to meet. Therefore, the sage wears coarse garb, but carries precious jade under his garment.

【注释】

则：效法。**贵**：可贵，这里引申为难得，稀少。奚侗曰："世之知我者少，是我独异于人，而为天下贵矣。"**褐（hè）**：古代贫苦百姓穿的粗布衣服。比喻贫贱的生活。**玉**：比喻美好的才能。班固《白虎通义》："玉者象君子之德。"成语："被褐怀玉"出于此。意谓穿粗布衣而怀揣美玉，比喻人有美德，深藏不露。后来这个成语也比喻贫寒而怀有真才实学的人。

【译文】

理解我的人太少了，能够效法我的人更为难得。所以圣人虽然怀着美好的才能，却过着贫贱的生活。

知者不博，博者不知

He who knows does not show off his learning, and he who shows off his learning does not know.

知者不博，博者不知。

《老子》第81章

He who knows does not show off his learning, and he who shows off his learning does not know.

【注释】

知：同智，明智，也可解为见解，知识。《商君书·更法》："有独知之虑者，必见骜于民。"**博**：广，多，广泛地学习。《礼记·中庸》："博厚所以载物也。"

老子这句话也有人解释为："有知识的人学问不广博，学问广博的人反而没有知识。"这样说也不无道理。但"有知识的人"和"学问广博的人"相对似和"信言"与"美言"，"善者"与"辩者"不合。

【译文】

明智的人不广求知识，广求知识的人不明智。

知者不言，言者不知

He who knows does not speak, and he who speaks does not know.

知者不言，言者不知。

《老子》第56章

He who knows does not speak, and he who speaks does not know.

【注释】

知者不言：真正得道之人并不多讲话。知者，一指智慧，见张松如《老子校读》，一指“道”，见许抗生《帛书老子注释与研究》。

【译文】

懂得道的人不夸夸其谈，夸夸其谈不是得道之人。

知足不辱，知止不殆

Whoever is contented will meet no disgrace, and whoever knows when and where to stop will meet no danger.

知足不辱，知止不殆，可以长久。

《老子》第44章

Whoever is contented will meet no disgrace, and whoever knows when and where to stop will meet no danger. And thus he is able to endure long without worry.

【注释】

知足不辱，知止不殆（dài）：知道满足就不会遭受侮辱，知道适可而止，就不会遇到危险。殆，危险。也省作知足、知止。后“知足不辱，知止不殆”作为成语流传下来。宋·苏轼《黄州安国寺记》：“寺僧曰继连，为僧首七年，得赐衣，又七年，当赐号，欲谢去，其后与父老相率留之。连笑曰：‘知足不辱，知止不殆。’卒谢去。”亦作“知止不辱，知足不殆。”

【译文】

知道满足就不会因需求过度而受到侮辱，知道适可而止就不会因过分贪求而遇到危险，只有这样才可以长寿久安。

知足者富，强行者有志

He who is content is rich; he who acts with persistence has will...

知足者富，强行者有志。不失其所者久，死而不亡者寿。

《老子》第33章

He who is content is rich; he who acts with persistence has will; he who does not lose his roots will endure; he who dies physically but preserves the Tao will enjoy a long life.

【注释】

强行：坚持实行的意思。**不失其所：**不丧失其本性的意思。**死而不亡：**意即精神不死，永垂不朽的意思。这是老子讲精神修养的话，他认为“知足”固然重要，而“强行”尤其重要。

【译文】

知道满足的人是富有的，坚持力行才是有志气的人。不违背道的规律的人能够长久，身死而精神永存的人才算长寿。

治大国若烹小鲜

Governing a great state is like frying small fish (so frequent disturbance should be avoided).

治大国若烹小鲜。

《老子》第60章

Governing a great state is like frying small fish (so frequent disturbance should be avoided).

【注释】

烹(pēng):煎,煮。**小鲜**:小鱼。鲜,《说文》:"鱼也。"《韩非子·解老》:"烹小鲜而数挠之,则贼其泽;治大国而数变法,则民苦之。是以有道之君贵静不重变法,故曰:'治大国若烹小鲜'。"河上公注曰:"烹小鱼,不去肠,不去鳞,不敢挠,恐其靡也。"蒋锡昌曰:"夫烹小鱼者,不可扰,扰之则鱼碎;治大国者,当无为,为之则民伤。故云'治大国若烹小鲜'也。"

【译文】

治理国家就像煎小鱼一样。

治人事天莫如啬

For the rule of the people and the service of Heaven, there is nothing better than the principle of inaction.

治人事天莫如啬，夫唯啬，是谓早服。

《老子》第59章

For the rule of the people and the service of Heaven, there is nothing better than the principle of "inaction." Only by "inaction" can one be unhurried and get ready early.

【注释】

治人：治理人民。**事天**：对付自然。事，侍奉，对付。天，自然。**啬**（sè）：节俭。这里泛指清静无为，积蓄力量。《韩非子·解老》曰："书之所谓'治人'者，适动静之节，省思虑之费也。所谓'事天'者，不极聪明之力，不尽知识之任。苟极尽则费神多，费神多则盲聋悖狂之祸至，是以啬之。啬之者，爱其精神，啬其智识也。故曰：'治人事天，莫如啬。'"**早服**：早作准备。服，服从，遵循。

【译文】

治理百姓，对付自然，最好的办法是清静无为。清静无为就是及早遵循道的规律。

致虚极，守静笃

Try to the utmost to make the heart vacant, and be sure to hold fast to quietude.

致虚极，守静笃。万物并作，吾以观复。夫物芸芸，各复归其根。

《老子》第16章

Try to the utmost to make the heart vacant, and be sure to hold fast to quietude. All things are growing and developing, and we see thereby their circulation. Though all things flourish with a myriad of variations, each one will eventually return to its roots.

【注释】

致虚：做到内心虚寂寡欲。**守静**：坚持清静无为。**笃**（dǔ）：深，甚。**并作**：一齐生长起来。**以**：凭借。**观复**：观察万物的往复循环的情况。**芸芸**：众多的样子。**归根**：回归到自己的本原。根，出发点，这里指死亡。

【译文】

极力做到虚寂寡欲，彻底坚持清静无为。万物一齐生长起来，我（凭借清静寡欲的品质）观察它们往复循环的情况。天下芸芸万物，最终都要回归到自己的本原。

重为轻根，静为躁君

The heavy is the root of the light, and the tranquil is the master of the active.

重为轻根，静为躁君。

《老子》第26章

The heavy is the root of the light, and the tranquil is the master of the active.

【注释】

躁（zào）：动。**君**：主，引伸为根本。

老子在这一章中，举出重与轻、静与动（躁）两对矛盾，并指出“重为轻根，静为躁（动）君，”本章终了又说：“轻则失根，躁则失君。”他认为轻与重对立，而重是矛盾的主要方面；动（躁）与静对立，而静是矛盾的主要方面。这是老子朴素的辩证法思想。作为事物发展变化的永恒规律来看，运动是绝对的，静止是相对的。老子由于受到他所处的时代和阶级的局限，还认识不到这一点。

【译文】

重是轻的基础，静是动的根本。

自见者不明，自是者不彰

He who only relies on his own eyes cannot see clearly; he who considers himself always in the right cannot tell right from wrong.

自见者不明，自是者不彰，自伐者无功，自矜者不长。

《老子》第24章

He who only relies on his own eyes cannot see clearly; he who considers himself always in the right cannot tell right from wrong; he who boasts himself will be given no credit; he who considers himself superior is not qualified for leadership.

【注释】

本章开头老子用“企者不立，跨者不行”作比喻，说“自见”、“自是”、“自伐”、“自矜”的后果都是不好的，不足取的。这些轻浮、急躁的举动都是反自然的，短暂而不能持久的。急躁冒进、自我炫耀，反而达不到自己的目的。此章内容和第22章“不自见，故明；不自是，故彰；不自伐，故有功；不自矜，故长。”互相对照就容易理解了。

【译文】

好自我表现的人反而不能扬名，好自以为是的人反而名声不能彰显。自夸的人反而没有功劳，总爱高人一等的人反而不能处人之上。

图书在版编目(CIP)数据

老子说 / 蔡希勤编著 .—北京：华语教学出版社，2006
(中国圣人文化丛书 . 老人家说系列)
ISBN 978-7-80200-215-9

Ⅰ. 老… Ⅱ. 蔡… Ⅲ. 汉语—对外汉语教学—语言读物
Ⅳ.H195.5

中国版本图书馆 CIP 数据核字(2006)第 071860 号

出版人：单 瑛

责任编辑：韩 晖　　封面设计：胡 湖

印刷监制：佟汉冬　　绘　　图：李士伋

老人家说 · 老子说
蔡希勤　编注
*

华语教学出版社出版
(中国北京百万庄大街 24 号　邮政编码 100037)
电话：(86)10-68320585
传真：(86)10-68326333
网址：www.sinolingua.com.cn
电子信箱：hyjx@ sinolingua.com.cn
北京松源印刷有限公司印刷
中国国际图书贸易总公司海外发行
(中国北京车公庄西路 35 号)
北京邮政信箱第 399 号　邮政编码 100044
新华书店国内发行
2006 年（32 开）第一版
2007 年第一版第二次印刷
2009 年第一版第三次印刷
(汉英)
ISBN 978-7-80200-215-9
9-CE-3732P
定价：29.80 元